THE SPICE FILES

Also available in this series:

THE METALLICA FILES
THE KURT COBAIN FILES
THE MARIAH CAREY JOURNAL
THE MADONNA DIARIES
THE LOST FAB FOUR CHRONICLES
THE OASIS CHRONICLES

First published June 1997
Copyright © RDO 1997

Published by
Arrowhead Books
Suite 201 - 37 Store Street
London WC1E 7BS.

All rights reserved. No part of this publication may be reproduced, stored in a retrieval system, or transmitted in any form or by any means electronic, mechanical, photocopying, recording or otherwise, without prior written permission of RDO.

Every effort has been made to trace the ownership of all copyright material and to secure permission from copyright holders. In the event of any question arising as to the use of material, we will be pleased to make the necessary corrections in future printings.

ISBN 1 901674 06 1 (WITH DOUBLE C.D.)
ISBN 1 901674 20 7 (WITH VIDEO)

CATALOGUE NO: AHB1100013 (WITH DOUBLE C.D.)
CATALOGUE NO: AHB2100020 (WITH VIDEO)

Printed and bound in the UK
by Bath Press

CONTENTS

1 INTRODUCTION
2 THE EARLY LIFE
3 THE SPICE FILES
4 QUOTES
5 INTERVIEW
6 CANNES
7 IN CONCLUSION

INTRODUCTION

Girl bands, don't ya just love 'em? Of course you do. We all do. We can't live without them. You were just practising your basic worship tactics when those Take That posters first covered your wall, knowing that they would one day be replaced by objects of a higher love. I know I did. And finally, after years of waiting for Bananarama to resurface, a group of girls has appeared in a supernova of publicity to recapture the attention so cruelly wrested from them by those strutting peacocks in designer shirts.

The frisky fivesome have hammered their way into our brains to become what they are today: a mega-group of epic proportions, ripping open the ribcage of nation states, and with painted nails, stealing the heart of a generation like no band since...dare I say it...The Beatles? Maybe that's going a bit too far, but then that's what they are all about. Going all the way, in the best tradition of the English Rose. Hang on a minute...

You want to know more about them. Don't we all? Despite all the media hype, the girls themselves are an enigmatic bunch. Perhaps that's part of the reason they're so much in demand, as they represent a femininity that is both on show to all but also secret and hidden from close scrutiny. That's why the tabloids are willing to pay thousands of pounds for every tiny scrap of information that they can muster about the Spices. And why you're flicking through this book!

The girls themselves don't much go in for detailed interviews. Catching one of them on her own is a major battle in itself, as it seems that they will only talk to the press as a group. As on stage, so in life. Whenever they do consent to appear in public, it's always as part of a carefully-choreographed photo-opportunity. What does this have to say about their commitment to Girl Power, to the independence they so loudly support? Maybe lots. Maybe nothing. Strict management of the talent is very much the way to do things these days. Take That were no different, nor come to think of it are established artists like U2 or Michael Jackson. The mystique and the inaccessibility all add to the image of beings who are above us mere mortals. That's showbusiness, kid.

Even a hardened cynic like myself has to take a subjective view on these matters. The sheer speed of their rise to the top has taken everybody by surprise, most of all the music press who are used to groups climbing quickly - but not this quickly. First song number one, first album number one, both staying there for weeks and not just in England - countries as far afield as Thailand and Venezuela have embraced the Spice phenomenon and made "Wannabe" their single of choice when it came out. In the space of just a few short months, they have conquered all opposition and are the hottest act in town wherever they go. Short of going on a stadium tour, they will not reach any more people than they have done already. Where next?

With a start as good as this, it doesn't matter. Whatever they do will be gratefully received by a fanbase which has quickly established itself in the wake of what has become the most successful PR job in recent times. The Spice Girls are a force to

be reckoned with, their very name entering the public consciousness to become a byword for any form of forwardness. In any paper you care to mention there has at one time or another been a Spice-related headline, sometimes on a daily basis.

For all the wannabes out there striving to copy those fancy dance routines and buying the same dresses, the message is crystal clear: you can do it too if you have the attitude. None of them are exceptionally beautiful or talented on their own. They're the sort of girls you'd catch in a club on any night of the week. The only difference is that when they get together, they become more than the sum of their parts to make up a group capable of taking on the world and winning. If you can explain this to anyone, then come to me first so we can do the same thing ourselves!

For now it's easiest to take a back seat and just marvel at the wonder of it all. At a time when the country was still in the final death throes of Conservative rule, a band of working-class girls touting the national flag managed to come up with something totally unique, the first group to take advantage of it's all-girl status rather than be defined by it. A few women who seem to have formed a real circle of friends rather than conform to the stereotype image of the manufactured band, which they are just beginning to shake off. For while it's no lie to say that they are singers and dancers who took part in a nationwide audition for the privilege of being in the group, it cannot be said that they are a bunch of industry puppets at the beck and call of male managers.

Or can it? And would it really matter if it was true or not? Would you like them any the less? Of course not. Would their message come across any differently? No. In these cynical times, it's nice to just take things at face value for a change, without looking for cracks in the fortress wall. Sometimes a Spice is just a Spice, as Freud would have said had he ever read The Sun. So forget the hype, forget those snobbish NME readers who wouldn't know a mass market if it hit them on the nose and forget you ever doubted their lasting appeal. Prepare to be lost in Spice....

2
THE EARLY LIFE

A long, long time ago in a galaxy not far from Woking, England, Chris and Bob Herbert were sitting around wondering how to keep their management business afloat. The company was called Heart and ideas were thin on the ground. It was 1994 and Take That were at the peak of their fame everywhere but America, record labels were falling over themselves to copy the premise and new boy bands were rehearsing and cutting demos for all of them. The idea of the girl group had, it was felt, been tried and found wanting. Shampoo had gone down a storm in Japan but bombed elsewhere, while female performers were typically the token sex-symbol in other line-ups.

Chris had other ideas. He felt that an all-girl Take That was going to be the next big thing and set about creating one from scratch. He put up flyers in the dance schools and drama colleges asking for young girls who can sing, dance and have an attitude. In reply came four hundred hopefuls, among them only three of the girls we know today - Mels B and C, and Victoria. They were given little reports and marked out of ten for their auditions, one comment famously noting that Victoria had bad skin. Less slap and more Nivea, Vicks! Those three and a girl called Michelle Stephenson made the final shortlist of ten girls who were invited to a second audition.

At this point Geri was still out of the picture, as she had been at a modelling shoot on the day of the first audition. Using a bit of her renowned girl power, she pestered Chris until he let her have a go. Although older than the others in the line-up and not quite as accomplished a stage performer as any of the other girls, she had that special something which Chris just had to put in the band. Asked how old she was, she cheekily retorted "I'm as old as you want me to be!" No points for originality Geri, but ten out of ten for style. And that was that, the girls were to start rehearsing in earnest. Story over. Er, except for Emma who hadn't joined yet.

Michelle was a good singer and all-round performer. All the crew reckoned she had the best voice. But whereas the other girls all gelled when they were thrown together, there was something notably lacking in the Spice department when it came to Ms. Stephenson. It wasn't just that she was a bit quiet and reserved, as all the girls claim to be this way in private, it was just that indefinable quality that the other girls had but she didn't. As they have gone on to show, it's not something you can fake or add on in a studio. It's Spice, and if you knew what made it happen you'd be rich. Sadly for Michelle this deficiency was fatal to her career and she was out. Or there is the alternative story that she got a university place and went off to care for her sick mother. She went on to appear in the press, saying that it never bothered her and she was happy with the choices she had made. Another hopeful made it on to the Richard and Judy show (a popular UK morning program), one of the girls who had made the final ten. She had been on her way down to London to the second round but let superstition get the better of her when a dodgy train connection was late. This was apparently a sign that she should go back home and try for another band. Yeah, right! The Spices might read their horoscopes but they don't let it rule their lives. If you see a black cat cross your path, stroke it. If you see a ladder, walk under it! If you think otherwise, you're not Spice and you'd better stop trying.

More auditions were held and little Emma (who is actually the same height as Geri) made it through. The flirty five were whisked off to the Woking studio where they were told the harsh facts by the people at Heart management. There were not going to be any limousines, no flash clothes, no film premieres and no star lifestyle for the foreseeable future. They were to basically sign their lives away for the time being and devote themselves to their work and if they didn't like it, then there were a few hundred others who would step in at a moments' notice. It wasn't as easy a decision as you'd expect, because all of them could easily have found other work the next day that would pay pretty good money.

Of course, I don't need to tell you that they all agreed. On June 7 that year Chris put them up in a hotel and put them through their paces, which was not a pretty sight. Geri couldn't dance much, none of them were quality singers and they had only just met, so they weren't working as a group. Months of hard work were ahead for the finished product to be released, but even after a few days together everyone was agreed - they had something special on their hands. The girls decided to fully commit themselves after Chris had laid it on the line - it was all or nothing for everyone.

They moved to Berkshire and lived in a house in Maidenhead, where Chris rented a provincial studio for a knock-down hundred pounds a week from a chap called Ian Lee, who would help form the girls' early sound. It was a far cry from a hundred pounds per hour 24-track recording suite, but it was a start. The girls would travel to and from the studio by bus every day, caching the odd bite to eat when they could. They were paid living expenses but nothing else. Gradually, they put together the songs and the dance routines with the help of professional choreographers, voice coaches and songwriters.

Mel B and Geri quickly proved themselves to have the dominant personalities and would often have conflicting ideas about what to do with the group, which led to some serious catfights. This didn't stop them going out clubbing together every weekend, though! Geri had very definite ideas about where to take the group and would think nothing of approaching industry figures or driving for hours to see a writer she knew would bring something good to the group. It was one of these outside writers, Tim Hawes, who probably gave them their biggest helping hand - he had written a song with the somewhat derivative title of "Sugar And Spice", which the girls loved. Chris had already thought of the name "Touch" which, in all honesty, was no good. Inspired by the song, the girls planned to rename themselves just "Spice", but as luck would have it another performer, a rapper, had already cornered the market on that one. "The Spice Girls" was a logical progression and was duly decided on.

They had the name, the look and the music to go all the way. Private shows to industry bigwigs convinced them they had what it took but sadly Chris was never to fully capitalise on his investment, as they promptly signed to Simon Fuller (manager of Annie Lennox), before going public. He got them a two million pound deal with Virgin Records. More than a year after that first audition, their first single was released under the watchful eye of Virgin execs and "Wannabe" went on to top the charts for eight weeks in England and beat off the opposition across Europe and beyond. The Spice invaders had arrived and were taking no prisoners.

3

THE SPICE FILES

Who are they? Where did they come from? Where are they going? From which deep, dark subconscious well of repressed emotion did they spring from? Who cares, because instead we've prepared these handy little anorak guides to each of the girls. Okay, so they don't tell you how tall Geri is without her platforms (five foot two on a good day if you're interested) or what colour Mel B's eyes are behind her famous specs (brown) or what make of sanitary device Mel C uses (what are you, some kind of sicko?). But they will provide a handy cut-out-and-keep guide to the girls. Not that you'd want to cut them out of course, because you already have the book and you don't want to go about cutting up your own stuff, do you? That would be foolish.

So here's the lowdown on the Spice Girls, from the heels of their fancy footwear to the ends of their perfectly plucked brows. Each brings their own unique angle to the group with their disparate backgrounds, yet somehow it all slams together to make something that works. That they have stayed together this long after being thrown together that day in an audition studio is proof of their approach to life - straight-up say-what-you-think honesty which has held them together this far, through all the long months of training, rehearsing and touring. They are all living proof of Girl Power in action, having got where they are today by pure effort.

NAME:	Emma Lee Bunton
BORN:	Jan 21, 1975 in London
STAR SIGN:	Aquarius
CLOTHES:	Love those babydolls, Emmie! The pigtails top off her sweet'n'spicy image which can be found at her favourite shops - Miss Selfridge, Kookai and Karen Millen. Hinting at her wild side are big army boots which can sometimes be found lurking under those cutesy dresses, with just a pair of pop socks to cover the dainty feet of Baby Spice.
HATES:	Being away from home and out of contact with beloved mumsy, showbiz blokes, insincerity, badly-baked doughnuts.
LOVES:	Being home, chatting with her mum, all things cuddly and fluffy, sweeties and chocolates and icky wikkle bunnies with puffy tails called mopsy and flopsy - but seriously, Emma's not quite the sheep among wolves she claims to be. She does like Dexy's Midnight Runners, after all.
FAVE MAN:	Film-star-type Johnny Depp and Michael French, dastardly David Wicks of Eastenders fame.
THEY SAY:	"I would have thought that she was all sweet and innocent, but she's not really. She just likes having a laugh and taking the piss out of herself and everyone." - Mel B "She's really, really grown. I think you change a lot between eighteen and twenty-one and she's really matured." - Geri "She's a lot more grown up now, but she's still a baby in the sense that she needs lots of attention and cuddles and things like that." - Victoria "Even though she's twenty-one now, she's still our baby because she's the youngest. Sometimes though, you'd think she was the eldest because she shouts at us and tells us we're being silly." - Mel C
SHE SAYS:	"I feel very comfortable in the group now, but people still think I'm shy. I guess that's the Baby Spice thing, but that name only stuck because I love wearing my baby dolls. I love my mum and I love spending time in my bedroom. That's no act, because none of us pretend to be something we're not."
PRE-SPICE:	Emma has been in the biz for years, ever since she was a toddler. She's been a child model most of her life and had only just come out of the prestigious Sylvia Young drama school when she joined the Spices. She also followed her mother into the martial arts and has a blue belt in karate.

NAME:	Melanie Janine Brown
BORN:	May 29, 1976 oop north in Leeds
STAR SIGN:	Gemini
CLOTHES:	Jean-Paul Gaultier for his mad ethnic look, but anything good - as long as it fits her style, it doesn't matter where it's from.
HATES:	The nine-to-five lifestyle, salad, anything organised, rules, false northerners, ra-ra skirts, her old boyfriend who sold their story to the papers, weak men.
LOVES:	Nelson Mandela, freedom to do what you want, Mr Chippy's fish'n'chip shop in Leeds, Leeds of course, the words Higgeldy Piggeldy and Hotch-Potch, going out clubbing, tattoos and other forms of body art, scaring people, chaos.
FAVE MEN:	George Clooney from ER, Will Smith from The Fresh Prince Of Bel Air.
THEY SAY:	"Big hair, big mouth - at least she's matching!" - Mel C "She used to say something without thinking about the consequences, but now she won't do that." - Victoria "She's matured and chilled out a little bit now. She's a lot more relaxed and laid back." - Geri "I love chatting to her. I go round to her house quite a lot. We just sit and talk about crap really." - Emma
SHE SAYS:	"You can get away with anything as long as you're cheeky." "I'm the one with the big hair and every band needs big hair." "I hate the way that some people try and conform, just because they're scared that they're going to make a bad impression. I say: just do it! It'll work out good in the end if you do it with a nice positive smile on your face." "I want to experience as much as possible. If I don't have a mad time and live the life then how the hell will I know if I like it or not?" "I liked detention at school because all the naughty ones got left together and it was like a riot."
PRE-SPICE:	Mel has always been in for the showbiz life. Her debut was at the tender age of six, where she played an American clown for the school drama. She studied contemporary dance at college where she also trained to be a drummer. She first hit the papers when she won a beauty competition to become Miss Leeds Weekly News. She supported herself with various jobs before hitting the headlines and has been a telesales girl and starred in provincial panto.

NAME:	Victoria Adams
BORN:	April 17, 1975 in Hertfordshire
STAR SIGN:	Aries
CLOTHES:	Surprise surprise, Posh Spice loves those labels and won't be seen dead in high street stores. Prada, Gucci and Plein Sud all enjoy her custom, although for a lover of the little black dress she doesn't frequent Jean Muir much. She'd love a Princess Di ballgown to impress the peasants!
HATES:	Japanese food - raw fish is for seagulls, guys! Meanness in any way, shape or form. Shabby dressers, poor hygiene, bad perms, school.
LOVES:	Need I say expensive clothes - Victoria cannot be without an extensive wardrobe at her disposal and is never seen out of her designer frocks. Not for nothing is she known to the world as Posh Spice. This follows on to her main love, which is of course shopping, shopping and more shopping!
FAVE MAN:	Latin Lover Antonio Banderas, star of Desperado and Evita. And Richard O'Brien for his sartorial elegance!
THEY SAY:	"I know she has the same sick, perverse humour as me. It's great!" - Mel B "She's become a lot more independent and she's grown. She's got a lot more attitude about her now. She's always had it in her, but now she's a lot more expressive, which is good." - Geri "She's not posh! She might wear posh clothes, but she's just as common as the rest of us!" - Mel C "I'm always ringing her for advice on what to wear. I like going out with her because she goes to posh places! When you catch her on a funny day you won't stop laughing. She's got a really dry sense of humour." - Emma
SHE SAYS:	"My favourite word is 'bollocks'! It's so expressive." "I love what I do, even if some people think I look miserable in photos because I don't smile much. That's not me looking miserable, that's me trying not to look too cheesy."
PRE-SPICE:	Vicky was the most academic of the girls - which isn't saying much - and had a normal school life. Something in her must have wanted to be a star, because she left and took up dancing seriously. She has toured with theatre companies and gone to stage schools, earning her way as a dancer and has been in a band before, singing cover versions of eighties stars.

NAME:	Geri Estelle Halliwell
BORN:	August 6, 1972 in London
STAR SIGN:	Leo
CLOTHES:	With her glam-rock coats, Union-Jack mini and whopping great platforms, Geri is clearly keen on the seventies look - the decade that taste forgot! Her bulging closet is a goldmine for outrageous costumes so Geri can slip into character for the day.
HATES:	School (she had a tough time as the only rebel in an all-girl establishment), tabloid photographers (scum of the Earth!), negativity, narrow mindedness, hypocrisy, smelly men!
LOVES:	Forward women, Margaret Thatcher ("but I'm not a real Tory"), tattoos (she has a new one on her arm where her Jaguar used to be - just the words "Girl Power"), Rod Stewart in his leopardskin trousers.
FAVE MAN:	Noel Gallagher, Liverpool football ace Patrick Berger and Kevin Phillips of Watford. Those shorts have a lot to answer for.
THEY SAY:	"She's always been the bossy bigmouth - and she's still the same! No change there." - Mel C "Geri's a bit mad, but she's really good when you want advice about something or want a shoulder to cry on. And a lot of the time she and I are the only ones who'll stay up all night for a party. We're not usually the party animals, but really, deep down maybe we are!" - Emma "I still think she's a nutter. She hasn't changed!" - Mel B "When I first met her, I thought, who is this nutter in mad clothes? Now I'm used to it, she seems really normal to me. Every time she used to say something, I used to feel a bit scared to say anything back, but now I just shut her up if I want to." - Victoria
SHE SAYS:	"I've always thought of myself as the Artful Dodger out of 'Oliver!', blagging my way through life. I was managing to talk my way into clubs long before I was in the band and I suppose I sort of talked my way into Spice Girls too. I'm not a trained singer or dancer, but I knew that I could bring some spirit to the group, some girl power."
PRE-SPICE:	Being older than the other girls, Geri's had a wide range of jobs before landing her dream ticket. She's been a game-show hostess, a club dancer, a model and, as everyone knows, she has been known to remove items of clothing for the camera...

NAME:	Melanie Jayne Chisholm
BORN:	Jan 12, 1976 in Widnes, near Liverpool
STAR SIGN:	Capricorn
CLOTHES:	For her trademark backflips, Sporty Spice needs room to move so no fancy frills for her on stage. She's moved away from her early look which had her wearing sports gear exclusively and can now be seen in trendy exercise threads from Dolce and Gabana. She likes to flaunt her tattoos as well, so hipsters and tank tops can both find a home in her wardrobe.
HATES:	Rudeness, smoking, faithless people.
LOVES:	Liverpool FC, all sports in general except golf, Flash Gordon, dancing, Madonna, Brookside (the scouse accents remind her of home).
FAVE MAN:	Liverpool footballer Jamie Redknapp ("when he speaks to me I go to pieces") and Die Hard star Bruce Willis.
THEY SAY:	"She's really blossomed into a babe!" - Geri "She's still the most disciplined and the strongest in spirit and determination. She never panics." - Mel B "She's come out of herself. She's not as quiet as she used to be. That's the main difference." - Victoria "She's my buddy. We drive to work together because we live nearby and I see her a lot at weekends. I can truly say I would trust her with my life. She's a babe. My friends all fancy the others, but they fall in love with Melanie C!" - Emma
SHE SAYS:	"I'll always remember how fate took a hand in my life. I was down to the last five for a role in 'Cats' and couldn't go to the audition because I had tonsilitus. They rejected me and then almost straight away I joined the Spice Girls, so how lucky was I?" "The music is probably the only thing I take seriously about my life. I listen to our album every now and again and although I'm dead proud of it, I can't help cringing when I listen to a couple of bits where I think the singing's a bit ropey."
PRE-SPICE:	Mel C has spent a long time waiting for her chance to be a star. She always wanted to be a pop star and follow in the footsteps of her mother, who had been a singer for some time and still gigs regularly. Mel is a classically-trained ballet dancer and once wanted to be a prima ballerina, but instead her singing talents lead her to a career as a session singer and to hundreds of auditions for stage roles before hitting the jackpot.

4 QUOTES

I know it sounds ungrateful but sometimes fame isn't that much fun. You're visiting all these fantastic places and you'll be sat there moaning "I want to go home!"

MEL C

"We had to do a shoot in a hot air balloon for a TV show at five o'clock in the morning and I had a hangover from hell! It was a nightmare. It was really cold and damp and early and we had to lie on the ground and be pulled up by the balloon. I was lying there with a pair of Gucci shoes on thinking, "It's five o'clock in the morning. It's freezing cold. I've got a nice new pair of shoes on and a nice suit on and I'm lying in some shitty field where cows have dunged everywhere. This is not rock'n'roll! I couldn't see Liam and Noel doing this." I was not impressed.

VICTORIA

We treat everyone the same because everyone wees and everyone dies. People think we're a bunch of bitches. But if you're a woman in this industry you have to shout louder than anyone else or people think you're stupid and easily manipulated. You can't win.

GERI

We've only had a bit of success so maybe it's good that we don't get sucked into the fame thing. If we stopped to think about it, we'd be in a mess.

EMMA

We're revitalising pop. Our songs are pop with intelligence and personality, unlike some! None of our songs are about wishy-washy love, unless it's about using a condom or summat!

MEL B

I was really pleased when we knocked Gary Barlow off the number one spot because I thought it was a reflection of our times. It was total Girl Power.

VICTORIA

We don't go to many showbiz parties, 'cos the music industry is not really our scene. We've met some celebrities but there's nothing special about them.

EMMA

We could be in the gutter tomorrow - that's the reality. What's unreal to me is that we've sold over three million copies of "Wannabe".

GERI

If my best friend's boyfriend came on to me I'd tell him where to get off - friends are far more important. It's one of those unwritten laws - thou shall not snog your friend's bloke.

MEL C

I watch Brookside because there's always loads of scandal in it and all the scouse accents make me feel better whenever I get homesick.

MEL C

I want a big house with a moat and dragons. Big dragons and a fort to keep people out!

VICTORIA

In the beginning my mum said "What is this, a religious cult or something?" And the truth is that that's how it's worked out, we're like a religious cult.

EMMA

Our house is mad. Emma is the longest in the bathroom, she spends hours faffing around. Mel C wants to watch football all the time and Vicki wants The Clothes Show on.

GERI

We're five individuals - we all dress differently but we've got real spirit and camaraderie that you only get between girls.

MEL B

Oops! Oh well, if you wear a dress like this you expect to reveal something. Anyway, everyone's seen them before, so I don't give a damn!

GERI at the Brit Awards

My grandmother always thought I was a nutter. When she saw the tattoo and tongue piercing she went absolutely mad. She said that if you pierce any part of your body you stop your whole spirit.

MEL B

I don't see myself as black. I don't see myself as white. I'm mixed, completely mixed, which means I've got the best of both worlds. A lot of mixed race people really kind of diss the white side of their family and I think that is so bad. You should never forget that this black person and this white person came together to make you, so you shouldn't disrespect any race or any colour. Many mixed race girls I speak to won't even go out with white guys or won't go out with black guys and I think that's really silly.

MEL B

Give us a few cocktails or champers and we'll probably dance topless on a table for you. At worst, we'd perform our five-girl moonie!

EMMA

When I meet anyone I don't see colour, I'm just me. I don't even think it should be an issue to talk about really, even though unfortunately you still have prejudice and you still have racism, which is crap. I don't feel as though I have to put on a black thing or a white thing or do anything else apart from just be myself.

MEL B

To have got this far by 20 seems like a miracle. I always dreamed of fame and a career in pop or showbiz so to have a taste of it at my age is a dream come true. I would never go solo. I love being in a band because it's like being with my five best mates and having a laugh every day. We're like sisters, I love them all so much.

EMMA

Whether it's good or bad, at least it's provoking thought somewhere. That's what the Spice Girls are all about; just getting everybody worked up to either ditch your boyfriend or go out and buy a new suit or just be exactly who you want to be. I'll say exactly what I think. I'm brutally honest.

MEL B

When things get written about me on a sexual level, I just think "You have got no idea." One of the first press pieces that came out about me insinuated that I'd had two in a bed or something! It was just so unbelievable. I just thought people are gonna pick that up and think, "Yeah right, as if!"

MEL B

My mum loves me being called Posh spice - she's hoping to become known as Posh Mum!

VICTORIA

All I'm bothered about is what's happening now. What message I can get across to young kids, how I can help my family, how I can make my life better and how I can make the people around me enjoy themselves. People in the public eye should never worry about what they're going to be doing in five years time. Who gives a shit what you're doing in five years time?

MEL B

I went to Antigua with my friend Janine who was three months pregnant. One day I made her go power-walking with me and on the way back she said, "Let's climb that mountain over there." Well, the mountain turned out to be a proper mountain. It was so steep I thought we were going to fall or slide down. Then I thought, "Oh my God, if anything happens to Janine I'll never forgive myself." But she was fine and even went jet-skiing later. She's certainly got girl power!

GERI

I really needed to go on holiday. It took around three days to clear the years' debris from my mind. It was like tidying my room in my mind, then my creativity was flowing freely. I wrote and wrote and wrote.

GERI

I went to Barbados with my mum, my brother and my boyfriend. There was nothing to do at night but I like that because I'm quite lazy. I just went to bed and watched telly. In the day I went to different beaches and sunbathed. The first day there I got really burnt on my chest and the top of my feet. It was funny because my mum does reflexology and she told me that the tops of your feet correspond to your chest!

EMMA

My first day on holiday, I went to the beach and heard Wannabe! There were loads of kids around the hotel pool listening to it and someone had said there was a Spice Girl around, so they were on the lookout for me. I wasn't wearing make-up, had my hair in a ponytail and was wearing a bikini. I thought, "Ah! They won;t recognise me because I look so rough." But then I found out that my dad had told everyone that his daughter was a Spice Girl. So then I had loads of photo-shoots around the pool - looking absolutely hideous!

VICTORIA

I had a fabulous time in St Lucia with my brother Paul, mum and step-dad. There wasn't a lot to do - it was like a health farm. So I just had loads of detox treatments, including one where I was scrubbed really hard with a loofah and salted oil. I was a bit sunburnt so it really hurt - I was yelping! And because of the salt and oil, I smelt like a crisp for days. I also had algae baths - bubbly baths with seaweed - and a seaweed wrap. They paint you in gunky green stuff, wrap you in cellophane and leave you for half an hour. I tried waterskiing and managed to stand up on the skis the second time. I thought I was doing well but my step-dad filmed me. When I saw myself on the video later, I realised I was totally crap. It took me a couple of days to unwind and chill out. Then I got all psyched up again and wanted to get back in to the swing of things. I got a bit bored having nothing to do.

MEL C

I went to Antigua with my mum, dad, sister and boyfriend. During the second week, we stayed with my grandma and visited my great-grandmother in Nevis. It was a bit too poncey for me there because they all sunbathe with their make-up on - and everyone stared at my G-string. But it was nice to see where my dad grew up and my grandma's house. She just lives off her land. It's a very pure way of life but I need my home comforts - my electrical things and my shopping. One night I met up with Geri at my hotel. She buried her head in the buffet and nobody noticed her.

MEL B

Whenever Jamie Redknapp speaks to me I go to pieces!

MEL C

I'm the minder. Me and Mel B compete to see who's the hardest - we're like the Gallagher brothers.

MEL C

I'm quite shy and find it difficult approaching people but when I went to see Liverpool recently I was determined to give John Barnes the Spice treatment. He's my hero but he came up to me and introduced himself to me first! I was amazed!

MEL C

At the moment my career is my priority but I don't want to be with anyone in the industry. I want to have un-popstar boyfriends. If I left my house looking a mess and a photographer took my picture I wouldn't care. That's what I look like when I buy the milk.

MEL C

We never mean to offend or hurt anybody. We're just a bit naughty. Eventually, it will probably get boring. And we don't want people thinking, "Oh, the Spice Girls are on telly again - I bet they had another food fight."

MEL C

I've got skin like a rhino. I've got a good sense of humour. I'm not at all embarrassed, why should I be?

GERI

Girl power is about doing exactly what you want to do, not about pleasing others. Posing topless was something I wanted to do at the time. I don't regret any of it.

GERI

Our philosophy is new-age feminism. You have a brain, you have a voice, you have an opinion, never be afraid to express yourself to the max. You can't beat attitude, intelligence and a wonderbra. It's a lethal combination!

GERI

If I set my mind to something I do it. My biggest wish for all of us is that we are happy, successful and that we stay true to ourselves.

VICTORIA

I bring warmth, affection and a high voice to the group.

EMMA

41

5

INTERVIEW

Number one in thirty different countries, a huge album and now standing tall (even Geri) over America as they become the first UK group to have a debut album and single at number one, the Spices have done it all. They've sold millions of records, done loads of videos, appeared on TV shows all over the world and captured the attention of every photographer in the land. We caught them not long ago when they appeared at the Prince's Trust Anniversary Concert in Manchester, where they met the Prince of the realm and gave a live show. We sent our bravest reporter to run the gauntlet of Spice power and bring back the goods on the girls, and they didn't pull any punches. You have been warned...

How did the concert go?

MEL B Great, thanks! Bloody marvellous. It's excellent being back in Britain.

GERI Yeah, good old blighty. We've been busy in America, touring around and meeting loads of people. We loved it, didn't we girls?

How do you like singing live?

MEL B Oh come on! We're not going to go through all that again are we? We can sing live and we can do it to a tape. Everyone knows you're doing it so you're not fooling anybody. You can't expect us to carry an orchestra with us all the time, can you?

EMMA I can't believe the things people have said. Like nobody's ever lip-synched before! It's our voices on the songs. That's us singing, that is!

Did you go on Saturday Night Live and David Letterman's show to prove it?

MEL C Well in a way, but it's not like there was some part of us that was saying 'come and have a go if you think you're hard enough'! It just suited us to do it at the time, and that's how they did things on those programs.

GERI We have wanted to do live shows all along, because that's part of what Spice Girls are about. We wanna be up there in front of the crowd, giving everybody what for at the top of our voices!

MEL B We want to shout at you!

You didn't fancy doing what Drew Barrymore did?

MEL B What was that then?

She stripped off live on Letterman.

MEL B [big laugh] No chance mate!

EMMA That's just a bit over the top, isn't it?

But you lot are supposed to get your kit off all the time.

GERI You mean I am!

MEL B Most of that stuff is made up by the press. I used to believe pretty much everything I ever read in the tabloids, but now I can't trust anything. They'll make anything up if they think they can get away with it.

VICTORIA If we want to wear revealing clothes, that's our choice. It's not to please any sad old men watching us and it's not because somebody's told us what to wear. If we want to show something, we show it!

EMMA I have read some things which are a bit true, I mean like the odd flash here and there. We don't make a habit of it though! You did a streak once, didn't you Mel?

MEL B Yeah, like a few yards down a corridor in a hotel! I don't flash me boobs out of taxis like some papers are saying.

GERI No, it's just me who does that.

Didn't Victoria once reveal all to some German tourists?

MEL B What are you so interested about this for? Are you some kind of pervert or summat?

VICTORIA Yes I did! So what?

GERI He's just jealous 'cos he'll never see it.

How do you explain your success in America?

MEL B There's nothing to explain. Girl power is a message for everyone, no matter where you live. It's relevant to everybody.

GERI We weren't very politically correct, were we? They aren't used to girls like us! It's all very weird, because we thought it was like, you know, land of the free and all that. We gave some people a bit of a shock.

MEL C They thought we were proper English ladies before we got there. We soon showed them! This businessman came up to us and said "I'm real pleased to meet you fine young ladies from England!"

MEL B And I said, "Whay-aye pet, we're dead chuffed to be 'ere an' all!" His face! He just went "Duhhh…"

GERI But they soon got us right. And now we've got them!

EMMA We are just so happy to have some hit records over there. Being the first ever British band to have their first single go number one is the best thing that's happened in a long while. I can't get over it. Spice Girls have arrived!

MEL B We had to do some funny old gigs there. We did this one in a fairground and there weren't that many people there, so it was a bit weird. But it was great going on Saturday Night Live and seeing all those comedians. I might do that one day, me.

GERI You a stand up?

VICTORIA Stood up more like!

MEL B F*** off!

EMMA You should see the poetry she writes.

Any good?

(All the girls except Mel B try not laugh at this point)

MEL B Well I bloody like that!

So much for solidarity.

MEL C Hey, watch it you or I'll punch yer lights out.

GERI She would an' all. Rock 'ard is our Mel C.

I don't doubt it! Does your success mean you'll be spending a lot more time in the States?

EMMA Not at the moment. We've got a lot to do between now and February next year. We've got a new album to write and that's gonna take up a lot of time. There's all sorts of other stuff we want to do which is going to mean things will get a bit quieter for a bit.

MEL B We're dead popular in Japan, but that doesn't mean we have to stay there all the time. That's why we have videos, stupid!

Was the President at any of your shows?

GERI I don't think so. If he was, he probably had loads of secret servicemen to stop us seeing him.

MEL B He probably didn't want us to corrupt his daughter!

Did you miss being away for the elections?

EMMA Not me. We all try to stay away from politics really.

Except Geri.

GERI Oh, for God's sake how many times have I got to say this? I'm not a Tory. I just said I admired Margaret Thatcher because she has ideals, and I admire people who have convictions that they stick with. I'm not saying like, 'elect Thatcher now!' I can't say anything without people getting the wrong idea. And even if I do say something I'm happy with, they just change it to suit what they want me to say! I can't win.

MEL B I'm a bit of an anarchist meself. It doesn't pay to get involved with politics.

But none of you complained much when the Conservatives claimed you were on their side.

GERI Well for a start, we were in America at the time and busy with the tour. When you're out there you either lose touch, or by the time you can say anything in return, you're too late. Sometimes it's just not worth the trouble. Besides, it didn't do them any good, did it?

So you're quite keen on Blair are you?

MEL B Who d'you think we are, Jeremy Paxman? They're all as bad as each other.

MEL C It's good to see a few more women MP's I suppose. Not so many grey suits.

GERI It'll make a change from the old lot. They were awful.

So you're not great fans of the establishment?

MEL B What I hate is this feeling that what you're doing all the time is wrong. If you wanna do something, do it! That's what we're all about. I don't want anyone standing over me telling me it's not a good idea to do this or that.

What about the monarchy?

EMMA You like that, don't you Geri!

GERI Cor, that Prince Charles. Phwoar!

MEL B She pinched him on the bum!

You pinched our future King? Good going!

GERI We were all together for this photoshoot and he was standing there next to us. I thought I had to do something 'cos I might not get another chance, so I went for it.

MEL B What did he feel like then?

EMMA I bet he had strong, firm cheeks.

VICTORIA He'll need them if he's gonna be sitting on a throne all the time.

MEL C Nah, I reckon he's all soft.

MEL B All wobbly!

GERI Actually, it was quite nice! I can't be mean, can I?

EMMA Not about Charlie.

VICTORIA Especially if you're going to be married.

GERI Yeah, that's right! [Geri flashes a huge ring on her wedding finger] Look! I'm married to Charles! Bow down to your queen, lowly hack!

You all have a talent for comedy. Did you get this from working for Comic Relief?

EMMA Oh, God, that was a mad night! We had so much to drink backstage we were dancing on the tables, then this guy says 'come outside, you've got to snog Johnathan Ross and Gryff Rhys Jones!'

MEL B We just went out and saw the crowd, and Johnathan was practically drooling...

GERI He was looking forward to it a bit, wasn't he? Dirty old man!

MEL C They were both lovely though.

MEL B Great blokes.

GERI I'd rather've snogged Jennifer Saunders though.

MEL B Only 'cos she looks like you, y'vain cow.

When I first saw the video for "Who Do You Think You Are?" I could hardly tell the difference myself.

GERI It was scary, wasn't it? She looked just like me and copied everything I did, all my little mannerisms. Weird!

VICTORIA It was great meeting them. Dawn French was really funny as me. She invited all of us round to tea and said that Lenny would do the cooking! We'll have to go there sometime.

MEL B They were all wonderful. It was a real treat to be in there with all those girls. They were like me - freaky misfits, loud and proud!

What brought about those new hairstyles in that video?

EMMA When Lulu came out I thought she'd have a fit, because she was all set to look like me with my pigtails and I'd just had my hair done all curly! She was okay, and probably looked more like me than I did that day.

VICTORIA It was the same with me - Dawn had hers in this bob and a sophisticated black dress, and there was me in my silver thing with a great long ponytail!

MEL C You were just scared no-one would spot the difference.

VICTORIA Outside, now!

MEL B [in heavy scouse accent] All right, calm down, calm down!

That's a bit more girl power.

MEL B That's what we're here for, to spread it about a bit.

GERI Maybe you are Mel, but we're a bit more choosy than you are.

MEL B You know what I sodding well mean. We're spreading the word, not our legs!

EMMA Girl power is where you know you can do it and nothing's going to stop you. It's about empowering yourself, not waiting around for someone else to do it for you!

So even boys can have girl power?

GERI They've had it too easy! The future is female, guys!

MEL B I don't want to say we're excluding boys from it, because we have just as many boy fans as there are girls. We just happen to be girls who know what we want and how to get it.

MEL C We want to be the ones who help blokes with their bags and go out drinking with our mates for a change.

VICTORIA We're saying whether you want to wear flash clothes or trakkie bottoms or nothing at all...

GERI Watch it!

VICTORIA ...You can do it. Don't ask anybody - except maybe your mum and your mates - and just go ahead. Whatever you want is right.

MEL C Within reason!....Usually.

6
CANNES

Cannes, for most of the year, is a big town like any other on the sunny continental coast. Flash hotels. Private beaches. Overpriced thimblefuls of coffee. But for a couple of weeks every year, it becomes a magnet for the film superstars of the world as they gather for the Cannes Film Festival. It's the one time of the year when the Hollywood set is forced to acknowledge that life exists outside of the USA, even if all it does is serve twiddly little canapes and direct really strange films with subtitles. This year was the biggest yet, the 50th Anniversary Special. Anybody who is anybody in the entertainment sector was there, from the lowliest bit-part actor to the all-powerful studio bosses - and the Spice Girls were no exception.

Now that they have the world's attention, they aim to keep it and appeared in a blaze of flash bulbs on the steps of the Palais Cinema, the biggest theatre in Cannes and traditional home of all the major premieres. They were there to announce that we would soon be able to see all of them at our local multiplex, because they're going to make a movie! Details are fairly fluid at the moment. Even the title is not set, but "Spice: The Movie" is currently the front runner. Original, huh? One thing is for sure - it's going to star the

Spices as themselves as we follow them through a week in their life, with a concert finale.

Previous pop stars have had mixed success with their big-screen offerings. Madonna has tried so many times to be good on film that the laws of probability alone meant that one or two can't be that bad. Finally with "Evita" she stuck to music and got it right, just as U2 did with "Rattle And Hum". The Spices plan to follow the lead of earlier stars like The Beatles and The Monkees, with films like "A Hard Day's Night" as the template rather than "Purple Rain". This means comedy and family laughs, so the girls are going to have to curb those caustic tongues of theirs if they want it to pass the censors' scissors! It's not going to be a true to life account by any means though, but a fictional jaunt through some set piece songs with a host of big stars appearing in cameo roles. At the time of press, the only name definitely linked is top British actor Richard E Grant, still best known for his role in eighties cult hit "Withnail And I". The lanky funnyman will take a starring role as the girls' manager! Asked whether Prince Charles will star, Mel B replied "We really enjoyed meeting Prince Charles but he won't be in the film. I cast him but he wasn't that good." None of the girls are worried about their chances of getting a knighthood then. Geri disappointed fans everywhere by adding: "We want children to like this film, so we are not going to be getting our kit off." Surely she can't mean that there are some

youngsters out there who would be offended by another glimpse of Her Spiciness in all her natural glory?

The ladies enjoyed a great time in France, attending all the big parties and showing off as usual. At a press conference they held court over a huge gathering of journalists, daring them to ask questions and ruthlessly putting them in their place before demanding that the massed ranks of paparazzi perform a Mexican wave. Who's manipulating who now, guys? The festival was a chance for the girls to flaunt their stuff for cameras everywhere, but the most raucous behaviour occurred behind closed doors, safely out of the way of the prying eyes of the press. They did a bit of table-dancing at Johnny Depp's Planet Hollywood party and retired to a private beach, where they performed a twenty-minute concert for French channel M6, the gallic equivalent of MTV. The American channel lost out on a scheduled session with the girls - a spokesman claimed it was over "creative differences" but the girls are keeping mum over their disagreement with MTV so far. Elsewhere they could be seen on a swanky 100ft yacht, kitted out in sunglasses and headscarves like real film stars, which they soon left to make a grand tour of the harbour in a speedboat. Reporters frantically tried to hire boats to go out for a closer look as the carefree five enjoyed yet more attention. Asked about their crazy stunts, a spokesman replied "They are high-spirited girls. Contrary to what people think, they're scarcely manipulated at all." So it must be true.

Elsewhere news continues to filter in from our extensive spy network. The Spices can already be seen on TV regularly, singing the praises of soft drinks in a dated eighties-look advert, from the marketing masterminds that brought us the blue Concorde (at Cannes, Victoria had her drink snatched from her lips because it was the wrong brand). The Pepsi sponsors are also backing a gig in Turkey which will be filmed in October, but rumours of an ITV special are "premature" say the band. The most interesting developments are in the girls' love lives, which have taken some knocks as they became ever more famous.

Geri's millionaire boyfriend Giovanni Laporta was given the shove after a few months. He made his pile in double glazing, but Geri's steamy reputation was too much for anything less than quadruple-thickness. The same fate was in store for long-term boyfriend of Emma, Mark Verghese. Victoria claims she ditched her fiancee soon after joining the group in a fit of girl power, but friends say they were already going their separate ways. The Posh One can now be seen with Manchester United and England midfielder David Beckham, but neither will confirm anything between them exists. Still, it doesn't do their reputations any harm, does it? The only Spice untroubled with romance is Mel C, who complains she can't find a boyfriend. Hello! Mel C! Over here, whenever you're ready! I can do next Thursday…

Mel B just hit the headlines with new squeeze Fjolnir Thorgeirsson, a 26 year-old businessman from hip'n'trendy Iceland, favourite country of Damon Albarn. She is supposedly just looking for a shoulder to cry on after splitting up from Richard Meyer, who according to the press is either a jewellery engraver or a car mechanic. Like all the dumped boys, he is claiming the break-up was 'amicable' and is carrying on with life as normal. Or as normal as it can be with a gang of reporters on your doorstep asking what the girls are like in bed, day after day after day. Fjolnir is, like all of the new boys, no stranger to the high life and has a considerable bank account of his own - though not as big as Mel's, which like the rest of the girls is already at three million smackers and could rise to as high as ten million on the back of the current deals alone.

With this amount on tap at your cashpoint, you could be forgiven for chucking it all in to take up a career as a full-time beach bum somewhere private and hot. Somehow, this image does not fit in with the raucous energy of the Spice Girls. They have barely been going for a year in the public eye after all, and show no signs of disappearing into the bargain bin of obscurity just yet. Queues are already forming for tickets to their world tour in 1998, which will see them spreading the word to fans in venues everywhere and merchandise with their name on it is selling like hot cakes all over the place. The future is Spicy.

7 IN CONCLUSION

The Spice bandwagon now stands at a major crossroads. Their exposure has probably just peaked in the UK and short of a Spice scandal will only build up momentum again as they start releasing new material, which will not be until we reach the next Christmas season. In the meantime, there is their forthcoming film to see which will probably be quite good as Richard E. Grant is in it as the girls' manager.

Christmas 1997 will probably be the moment they either consolidate their stranglehold over the record-buyers or start the inescapable slide down into B-list celebrity land and appearances on "Call My Bluff"! On present form, they will take it by a landslide. There is no other act like them around at the moment and while Take That had Boyzone, East 17 and a host of other boy bands to compete with, the Spices are currently the only big fish in the pond. The existence of these satellite groups only proves that there is a market for them, so it can only be a matter of time before there are a host of girl groups rushing in to fill up the gaps.

Being fans of Margaret Thatcher they should relish the challenge of some healthy free-market competition. If they carry on as they have done so far, they will stay on top until the end, just as TT did. That is the great virtue of making the first move in a tactical business like the music industry. Normally the only thing about being a pioneer is that you're the one who gets the arrows in the back, but for the girls it was a stroke of genius to hit the mainstream when they did.

Of course, the success or failure of a group doesn't necessarily ride on their timing. But it helps a lot. "Wannabe" was a summer hit, a season during which industry figures traditionally put out new songs by unknown artists or

weak ones from established names. This is a common tactic because the summertime is slow for everything in the media - repeats on television, everybody goes outside or on holiday and in general, fewer records are bought. Consequently, a large sales push can give a group a higher position than it would have otherwise achieved against the big guns over the Christmas period. Film releases are the exception to this rule, with blockbusters being released back-to-back over summer because nobody tends to buy films for Christmas.

This is nothing to be ashamed of. It's just business and many big acts started out with a hefty shove from their publishers. That the Spices are no exception should come as no surprise to anyone with any common sense, but...who cares? I mean, who really cares where it came from if it makes you feel good? If you want absolute authenticity in your musical environment then stick to pub gigs and make sure they don't play any cover versions while you're listening.

Musical complaints aside, Spice has proven to be a very marketable brand name. They have sold their name and image to a cornucopia of products that carry the Spice logo, with bootleg merchandising (the one sure sign that you're a star) appearing in all kinds of places. Assume nothing. If you haven't seen their name on it, just wait for a while. If you think you've heard too much about them already, you ain't seen nothing yet. With the arrival of the film, the new album and singles to go with it all coming out in late '97, they will be everywhere.

The secret of their success? Like all big groups, they appeal to a broad range of fans. Wherever they appear, you will see a cross-section of society turning up to see them, not just screaming schoolchildren - from toddlers to grannies, everyone benefits from a touch of Spice. In each girl's carefully-presented persona there is something to identify with, from innocent girly Emma to Earth-Mother Geri, so that no one is left out. The question of who is your

favourite Spice has entered the vernacular and pop psychologists claim your answer will reveal aspects of your personality. Say it is Victoria and you are an aspiring rich aristo. Mel B and you're a party animal. Obvious, but it works and with this appeal they have stealthily wormed their way into the public consciousness.

The girls are also human beings, who have been caught up in the whirlwind too. Life as a pop star is great, there's no doubt about that, but when you're this popular you have to put your social life on hold. You've got money at last but you can't spend it and heaven forbid you should try and have a meaningful relationship. Despite all their proclamations about being individuals with their own wants and needs and their much-vaunted friendship, they live in an open prison. It is their choice, so save your pity for the hundreds of girls who didn't make it through the auditions, but who at least can go to the pub without being mobbed.

Can they go on like this? Or are they just what's fashionable at the moment? The longevity of a pop group is notoriously short for most. Only a few bands or individuals have sustained their popularity for any length of time, either by resolutely sticking to their original image or constantly changing to fit the needs of the audience. The Spices now have a very definite image of their own which has a very high recognition factor, from the distinctive typeset of the logo to the hairstyle of Mel B. When Boy George cut his locks off, it made the papers so imagine what the reaction would be if Mel did the same! The opposite is also true - remain the same and you become a stereotype of yourself. Gary Glitter still rocks on in his flamboyant costumes like he did in the seventies and Tom Jones still packs the punters in at Vegas, because they have remained constant over the years. Take That knew they had to change and stepped out of the limelight while they made their last album, to return with a drastic image change. Gone were the smart haircuts and flashy clothes, in were grunge and dreadlocks. The same may well be

done with the Spices when they return with their new album. What can we expect? A roughed-up Victoria? A dowdy Geri and a Skunk Anansie-style skinhead for Mel B? Now that would be telling.

Whatever it is, they'll be the same girls underneath it all, with the same message that they have always projected. The 'Girl Power' drive for self belief and to out-lad the lads will remain, because it's their biggest selling point, far more important than the trivial matter of what they are wearing. Their attitude of girls against the world will continue to fascinate us all, who are plainly behind the times where sexual equality is concerned. Even though they acknowledge that they are led by male management, their up-front nature will continue to impress men and women alike, a welcome change from the egotistical ravings of a gangsta rapper or the anodyne ramblings from another boy band. They have Spiced up the music scene no end and for this alone we should be eternally grateful.

THE FACE

GIRL'S WORLD
The Spice Girls by
Peter Robathan

SPICE! ABOVE AND BEYOND

STAR WARS / PRINCE / MAGGIE CHEUNG / AEROSMITH / EELS / CARL CRAIG / SPRING

ACKNOWLEDGMENTS

Company executive - Richard Driscoll.
Arrowhead executive - David Richter.
Designed by Glenn Pamenter & Daniel Wilkins
Edited, copywritten + story by Michael Joseph,
David Richter & Ski Newton.

All photographs in this work are courtesy of Visual Entertainment Archives Inc., New York, U.S.A.